C000090073

Skills Builders

SB

YEAR 5

SPELLING AND VOCABULARY

Sarah Turner

Acknowledgements

Every effort has been made to trace all copyright holders, but if any have been inadvertently overlooked, the Publishers will be pleased to make the necessary arrangements at the first opportunity.

Although every effort has been made to ensure that website addresses are correct at time of going to press, Rising Stars cannot be held responsible for the content of any website mentioned in this book. It is sometimes possible to find a relocated web page by typing in the address of the home page for a website in the URL window of your browser.

Hachette UK's policy is to use papers that are natural, renewable and recyclable products and made from wood grown in sustainable forests. The logging and manufacturing processes are expected to conform to the environmental regulations of the country of origin.

ISBN: 978-1-78339-727-3

Text, design and layout © 2016 Rising Stars UK Ltd

First published in 2016 by Rising Stars UK Ltd
Rising Stars UK Ltd, An Hachette UK Company
Carmelite House 50 Victoria Embankment
London EC4Y 0DZ
www.risingstars-uk.com

All facts are correct at time of going to press.

Author: Sarah Turner
Educational Consultant: Madeleine Barnes
Publisher: Laura White
Illustrator: Emily Skinner
Logo design: Amparo Barrera, Kneath Associates Ltd
Design: Julie Martin
Typesetting: Newgen
Cover design: Amparo Barrera, Kneath Associates Ltd
Project Manager: Seonaid Loader, Out of House Publishing
Copy Editor: Claire Pearce-Jones
Proofreader: Jennie Clifford
Software development: Alex Morris

British Library Cataloguing–in–Publication Data
A CIP record for this book is available from the British Library.
Printed by Liberduplex S.L., Barcelona, Spain

MIX
Paper from
responsible sources
FSC® C109440

Contents

SPELLING

UNIT 1   **ai** sound spelled **ei**, **eigh** and **ey** 4

UNIT 2   **i** sound spelled **y** 5

UNIT 3   **u** sound spelled **ou** 6

UNIT 4   **g** sound spelled **gue** 7

UNIT 5   **k** sound spelled **que** 8

UNIT 6   **sh** sound spelled **ch** 9

UNIT 7   **s** sound spelled **sc** 10

UNIT 8   Suffix: **ly** 11

UNIT 9   Suffixes: **tion**, **sion**, **ssion** and **cian** 12

UNIT 10   Letter string **ough** 14

UNIT 11   Words ending in **cious** and **tious** 16

UNIT 12   Words ending in **cial** and **tial** 18

UNIT 13   Words ending in **able** and **ible** 21

UNIT 14   Silent letters 23

UNIT 15   Double letters 25

UNIT 16   Homophones and near-homophones 27

UNIT 17   Adding prefixes and suffixes 29

UNIT 18   Stress in words 31

UNIT 19   Etymology and word families 33

UNIT 20   Word lists 35

VOCABULARY

UNIT 21   Using a dictionary and thesaurus 37

UNIT 22   Idioms 39

UNIT 23   Antonyms 41

UNIT 24   Word meaning 43

UNIT 25   Vocabulary in context 45

Word lists 47

All of the answers can be found online. To get access, simply register or login at **www.risingstars-uk.com**.

1 ai sound spelled ei, eigh and ey

There are many ways to spell the sound *ai*.

Spelling	Examples
ai	brain, plain
ay	day, play
a_e	fate, plate
ei	vein, veil, feint
eigh	weigh, neighbour
ey	they, obey, prey

Activity 1

How many words can you find with these spelling patterns? One of each has been done for you. Copy the table into your book and add words to each list.

ei	eigh	ey
reins	eight	survey

Activity 2

Choose the correct spelling to complete each sentence.

a) To make a cake, you must _____ the ingredients. (wey/weigh/way)

b) Your blood travels through _____ in your body. (veyns/veins/veighns)

c) An octagon has _____ sides. (eight/eyght/aight)

d) My next door _____ has a pet dog. (naighbour/neighbour/nayebour)

e) The lorry was carrying _____ across the channel. (freight/frait/frate)

Investigate!

How many words can you find with the *ai* sound in? Use these words to create a wordsearch for a friend to complete.

2 i sound spelled y

There are many words with the short *i* sound in them. Most of these words are spelled with an **i**; however, some words have a **y** instead of an **i**.

Activity 1

Use the short *i* words from the list to complete the sentences below.

gym   hymn   crystal   lyrics

mystery   oxygen   syrup   system

a) Diamonds are a type of _____.

b) Everyone joined in the _____ singing.

c) I enjoy reading _____ stories.

d) You get fit by working out at the _____.

e) The Earth's atmosphere is one-fifth _____.

f) The song has very difficult _____.

g) Do you have _____ on your pancakes?

h) We are using a new computer _____ at school.

Activity 2

Can you find these words in the dictionary and use them in a sentence?

rhythm   cymbal   analysis   symphony   systematic

Investigate!

How many words can you find with the *i* sound spelled **y**? Can you create a clue for each word for a friend to solve?

3 u sound spelled ou

There are different ways to make the short *u* sound in a word.

Spelling	Examples
u	mug, rug
o_e	glove, love, some
ou	enough, touch

Activity 1

Unscramble the words in brackets ( ), which each have the short *u* sound in them, to complete each sentence.

a) Do not _____ the objects on display. (outch)

b) The room was full of _____ men. (ngyou)

c) _____ click to open the document. (boudle)

d) China is a _____ with a large population. (ntcryou)

e) My young _____ is coming to stay this weekend. (scoiun)

f) These plants will _____ in full sunlight. (sihfoulr)

Activity 2

Sort the words into the correct box for the sound made by the letters **ou**.

mourn   touch   tour   would   crouch   lounge   course
group   sound   country   mousse

ow (as in 'loud')	u (as in 'couple')	oo (as in 'route')	or (as in 'pour')

Investigate!

How many words can you think of in two minutes with the *u* sound spelled **ou**? Can you put them into a sentence to show what they mean?

4 g sound spelled gue

Some words that have a *g* sound at the end are spelled as **gue**.

league, fatigue, prologue

Activity 1

Use the words from the list to complete the sentences below.

plague	rogue	tongue	vague	dialogue	fatigue

a) That man is nothing more than a _____.

b) I have a _____ idea that I've seen her before.

c) There could be no agreement without further _____.

d) In the Bible, Egypt suffered a _____ of locusts.

e) _____ is extreme tiredness.

Activity 2

Write the definition of the following words.

a) league

b) epilogue

c) synagogue

d) colleague

e) monologue

Investigate!

Use the words from this unit to create a crossword with clues for others to solve.

5) k sound spelled que

Some words have a *k* sound at the end that is spelled **que**. Many of these words originate from the French language.

antique, oblique, opaque

Activity 1

Unscramble the words in brackets ( ), which each have the *k* sound spelled **que** in them, to complete each sentence.

a) _____ means the only one of its kind. (iqeuun)

b) I bought this dress at the new _____. (tiboeuqu)

c) Muslims pray in a _____. (qmoseu)

d) A wall _____ shows where the famous explorer lived. (uepaql)

e) I will pay for the goods with a _____. (ueqehc)

Activity 2

Use the words in the list to complete the sentences.

picturesque   grotesque   antique   technique

a) The _____ store had a lot of china for sale.

b) The old cottage looked _____.

c) _____ can mean very ugly.

d) The sportsman had an extraordinary _____.

Investigate!

Can you write a list of the words ending with the *k* sound spelled **que**? Are there any other words that have not been used already on this page?

6 sh sound spelled ch

There are many words in the English language that originate from other languages. This has an impact on the way we spell them.

Some words have a *sh* sound in them but are spelled **ch**. This is because the origin of most of these words is French.

chef, chic, chauffeur

Activity 1

Use a word from the list to complete each of the sentences below.

chalet   machine   brochure   parachute   chef

a) This washing _____ is the latest model.

b) The _____ cooked a fantastic meal.

c) The skiers rented a _____.

d) When the pilot ejected, his _____ opened.

e) Find the best holiday in our new _____.

Activity 2

Unscramble the words in brackets ( ) to solve the clues.

a) This is a girl's name. (celhleMi) _____

b) A man grows one on his face. (schemtuoa) _____

c) This is a famous place in America. (goChica) _____

d) You make this tart out of eggs. (icehqu) _____

Investigate!

How many words can you remember with the *sh* sound spelled **ch**? Use these words to create anagrams for others to complete.

7   s sound spelled sc

Some words that have an s sound in them are spelled with **sc**. This spelling originally came from Latin.

science, **scene**

Activity 1

Choose the correct word from the list to complete each of the sentences below.

science	scenery	scissors	descend	scented

a) The Rocky Mountains have some fantastic _____.

b) Kate loves to relax in a hot, _____ bath.

c) Astronomy is the _____ of the stars.

d) Good _____ need to be kept sharp.

e) To _____ is to go down.

Activity 2

Write the definition for each of these **sc** words.

Word	Definition
ascent	
crescent	
fascinate	
scent	
scene	

Investigate!

Use the words from this page to create a crossword with clues for others to complete.

8 Suffix: ly

The suffix **ly** is joined to an adjective to form an adverb.

There are some rules you need to remember when adding the suffix **ly**.

- For many words, just add **ly** to the end without any change to the root word.

  sadly, finally, usually

- If the root word ends in a **y** with a consonant letter before it, the **y** is changed to an **i** before adding **ly**.

  happily, angrily

- If the root word ends with **le**, the **le** is changed to **ly**.

  gently, simply, nobly

- If the root word ends with **ic**, **ally** is usually added rather than just **ly**.

  basically, dramatically

Activity 1

Copy this table into your book and add **ly** to each of the root words. Remember the spelling rules from above!

Root word	ly word
near	
grumpy	
scientific	
frantic	
noble	
rapid	
brief	
wicked	

Investigate!

Write a sentence using each of these adverbs: suddenly, carefully, angrily, usually, impatiently and unbelievably.

9 Suffixes: tion, sion, ssion and cian

There are lots of nouns that end with the sound *shun*. How do you spell them? Here are some spelling rules to help you work out which spelling of *shun* to use.

Spelling	When	Examples
tion	The most common spelling, including **ation**, **ition** and **ction**. Use these endings when the root word ends in **t** or **te**.	action injection
sion	Use when the root word ends in **d** or **se**.	expansion tension
ssion	Use when the root word ends in **ss** or **mit**.	expression permission
cian	Use when the root word ends in **c** or **cs**; these are often words for jobs.	musician magician

Activity 1

Sort these words into the correct *shun* ending from above.

invention   politician   expansion   confession

action   discussion   omission   television

demotion   exception   division   electrician

tion	sion	ssion	cian

What other words could you add to the table?

Activity 2

Add **tion** or **sion** to these words. Use the spelling rules to help you.

comple_____	accommoda_____
rela_____	dimen_____
commis_____	sta_____
protec_____	illu_____

Activity 3

Copy this table into your book. Use the *shun* suffixes to change the verbs into nouns.

Verb	Noun	Verb	Noun
permit		complete	
omit		inflate	
confess		remit	
extend		admit	
transmit		invent	

Activity 4

Complete the words in the sentences below by adding the correct *shun* suffixes.

a) She is a politi_____ and is on the televi_____.

b) His profe_____ is an opti_____.

c) I have an invita_____ to a party at a famous musi_____'s house.

d) The teacher gave permi_____ for the children to have an extra break.

e) The mathematic_____ was very quick at finding the answer to the problem.

10 Letter string ough

The spelling **ough** has lots of different sounds.

or, off, uff, oe, oo, ow and *u.*

It is a remnant of Old English spelling.

Sound	Example words
or	ought, bought, thought
off	trough, cough
uff	rough, tough, enough
oe	though, although, dough
oo	through
ow	plough, bough
u	thorough, borough

Activity 1

Use the words in the list to complete the sentences below.

though   bough   rough   through   cough   plough

a) He kicked the ball _____ the window.

b) The farmer _____ed his field.

c) Even _____ he was tired, he kept running.

d) The main branch of a tree is called the _____.

e) Shaz has an awful cold and _____.

f) The path was _____ and rocky.

Activity 2

Match the correct **ough** word to its meaning. One has been done for you.

Something that bread is made from.   fought
The word for the digit 0.   thorough
As much or as many as required.   dough
The past tense of fight.   enough
Done with great care and completeness.   nought

14

Activity 3

Draw lines connecting each **ough** word on the left with the word that it rhymes with on the right.

through	cow
cough	flew
though	puff
plough	off
enough	so

Activity 4

Use these rhyming pairs to write rhyming couplets. One has been done for you.

He sold his cow

To buy a plough.

Investigate!

Write a definition for the following words: bought, thorough, through, brought, though.

11 Words ending in cious and tious

Two of the suffixes to change nouns to adjectives sound like *shus*, but there are two possible spellings – **cious** is most common but some take **tious**. The noun usually suggests the spelling of the adjective.

- If the root word ends in **ce**, use **cious**. Delete the **e** and add **ious** to form the adjective adding **cious**.

  vice ⟶ vicious

  space ⟶ spacious

- If the root word has a **shun** ending, then **tious** should be added to form the adjective.

  ambition ⟶ ambitious

  caution ⟶ cautious

- **Suspicious** is the only **cious** word that has a noun with a **shun** ending.

  suspicion ⟶ suspicious

- Some adjectives ending **tious** don't have a noun form, so you will just have to learn these.

  conscientious, scrumptious, surreptitious

Activity 1

Copy the table into your book and write the adjective for each of the nouns by adding **cious** or **tious**.

Noun	Adjective
repetition	
space	
grace	
fiction	
superstition	
malice	

Activity 2

Complete each of the underlined words using **cious** or **tious**.

a) The girl was a very <u>conscien</u>_____ and hard worker.

b) She was very <u>ambi</u>_____; she wanted to be top of the class.

c) I thought the reasons he gave were completely <u>ficti</u>_____.

d) The table was full of <u>deli</u>_____ food.

e) Be very <u>cau</u>_____ when driving at night.

Activity 3

Write a definition for each of these words. Use a dictionary if you need to.

Word	Definition
malicious	
suspicious	
repetitious	
fractious	
unconscious	
ferocious	

Activity 4

Using the root word, create a word to complete each of these sentences.

a) The room was very _____. (space)

b) The disease seemed to be very _____. (infect)

c) The pupil was very _____ and wanted to get the highest score. (ambition)

d) I thought the reasons he gave were completely _____. (fiction)

e) The new cereal bar was _____ and good for you. (nutrition)

Investigate!

How many words can you think of in two minutes that end in either **cious** or **tious**?

12 Words ending in cial and tial

Some suffixes for adjectives sound like *shul*, but there are two possible spellings – **cial** and **tial**. Sometimes looking at the root word will give you a clue about which spelling to use.

For example, the **c** in **offi̱ce** tells you that the spelling for the suffix should be **cial**.

office ⟶ offi̱cial

The **t** in **presiden̲t** tells you that the spelling for the suffix should be **tial**.

president ⟶ presiden̲tial

Activity 1

Add these **tial** words to the following sentences. Use a dictionary to help you.

initial   confidential   influential   essential

a) The meeting was very _____.

b) The woman's speech was very _____ in changing the rules.

c) Exercise is _____ for good health.

d) My _____ reaction was amazement.

Activity 2

Draw a line to the correct **cial** word.

A birthday is a _____ day.   financial

During a space mission, oxygen is _____.   facial

Christmas has become very _____.   crucial

A holiday is a large _____ outlay.   commercial

The woman went to the salon for a relaxing _____. special

Activity 3

Do these adjectives end in **cial** or **tial**? Use your dictionary to complete each one.

a) ini _____

b) provin _____

c) unoffi _____

d) residen _____

e) essen _____

f) finan _____

Activity 4

Use the words in the list to complete the sentences below.

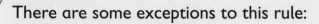

special   **artificial**   **essential**   **crucial**   **partial**   **facial**

a) His _____ expressions are comical.

b) There is a _____ album for the wedding photographs.

c) It was _____ that we won the match!

d) There was a _____ eclipse of the moon yesterday.

e) It is _____ that you go to school and learn.

f) The new football ground uses _____ grass.

There are some exceptions to this rule:

benefit ⟶ **beneficial**
palace ⟶ **palatial**

You will have to learn these words on their own!

19

Activity 5

Which suffix can be added to the following words?

tial   **cial**

a) offi_____

b) confiden_____

c) ini_____

d) so_____

e) superfi_____

Activity 6

Which suffix can be added to the following words?

tial   **cial**

a) impar_____

b) benefi_____

c) influen_____

d) mar_____

e) poten_____

f) spe_____

Investigate!

How many words can you think of with **tial** or **cial**? Use these words to create anagrams and clues for others to solve.

13 Words ending in able and ible

For most adjectives that end with the *able* sound, the suffixes are spelled **able**, and they have related verbs and nouns.

Verb	Adjective	Noun
adore	adorable	adoration
apply	applicable	application
consider	considerable	consideration
reason	reasonable	reasoning

As the suffix **able** starts with a vowel, you have to check the spelling.

• After a short vowel sound with a single consonant, double the last consonant.

• Drop the final **e**, except after soft consonants such as **g** and **c**.

• Change a **y** after a consonant to **i**.

There are fewer adjectives ending in **ible**, and they have less obvious roots.

possible, sensible, credible, visible, horrible, terrible

Activity 1

Use the words from the list to complete the sentences below.

comfortable   considerable   adorable   tolerable   reasonable   reliable

a) The bicycle picked up _____ speed going down the hill.

b) The cuddly puppy was utterly _____.

c) Those jeans were a _____ price.

d) My shoes are extremely _____.

e) Please keep the noise to a _____ level.

f) She is my most _____ worker in the class.

Activity 2

Match each of the words to its definition. One has been done for you.

Word	Definition
incredible	within one's powers
doable	possible and practical to do easily or conveniently
visible	difficult to believe; extraordinary
applicable	easily seen; clear or apparent
reliable	able to be endured
tolerable	consistently good in quality or performance; able to be trusted
noticeable	relevant or appropriate
feasible	able to be seen

Activity 3

Add **ible** or **able** to complete these words.

a) agree_____

b) dispos_____

c) ed_____

d) invinc_____

e) vis_____

f) forgiv_____

g) valu_____

h) recognis_____

i) cred_____

j) identifi_____

Investigate!

Can you use an **able** word to complete these clues?

a) If you notice it, it must be _____.

b) If it applies to you, it must be _____.

14 Silent letters

Several spelling patterns have silent letters, from their origins in older languages. We do not sound the silent letter when pronouncing the word. Here are some common silent letter examples.

Silent **b**	lamb, thumb, climb, bomb, doubt
Silent **c**	science, conscience, muscle, scissors, scene, fascinate
Silent **l**	calm, half, calf
Silent **n**	autumn, hymn, solemn
Silent **p**	psalm, pneumonia, psychology
Silent **t**	castle, thistle, whistle, listen, mortgage

Activity 1

These words all have letters that do not make any sound. <u>Underline</u> the silent letter in each word.

comb   gnome   fasten   wrap

wrong   listen   gnat   climb

gnash   knelt   sign   knuckle

wrinkly   Christmas   design   wrist

reign   know   knife   knock

limb   foreign   knew   numb

writing   christen   knowledge   kneel

Copy the table below into your book and sort the words in the list above into the correct column.

Silent b	Silent g	Silent t	Silent k	Silent w

Activity 2

Use the words from the list to complete the sentences below.

doubt   fascinating   subtle   asthma   silhouette   opossum

a) Harrison needs an inhaler because he has _____.

b) The jury were in no _____ that the defendant was innocent.

c) The children found the exhibition _____ and wanted to stay longer.

d) The _____ is a marsupial that lives in the western hemisphere.

e) The ice-cream had a very _____ flavour.

f) She could see the _____ of a fox in the darkness.

Activity 3

Write the missing word to complete the clues. All the words contain a silent letter.

a) _____ An insect that whines and bites.

b) _____ The beat in a piece of music.

c) _____ A tiny piece of bread or biscuit.

d) _____ You do this on a door to get an answer.

e) _____ An African wild animal with one big horn.

f) _____ The biggest mammal.

Investigate!

How many words can you find in your reading book that contain a silent letter?

15 Double letters

One of the most common problems with spelling in English is not knowing when a single sound is made by double letters.

Here are all the words from the word list for Years 5 and 6 that have double letters.

accommodate	communicate	guarantee	occur
accompany	community	harass	opportunity
according	correspond	immediate	profession
aggressive	embarrass	immediately	programme
apparent	equipped	interrupt	recommend
appreciate	especially	marvellous	sufficient
attached	exaggerate	necessary	suggest
committee	excellent	occupy	

Can you remember how to spell all of these words? Ask someone to test you on them.

Activity 1

Do these words need a double or single **t**, **l** or **s**? Complete the words below.

t	l	s
fla____er	leve____ed	di____cuss
pa____ing	trave____er	di____tress
ca____er	pane____ed	bo____ed
admi____ed	pi____s	me____ing
craf____ed	dri____ing	dre____ing
na____er	sti____ed	mi____lead
buffe____ing	sou____ess	flo____ing
fas____en	coo____ing	tea____ing
bloa____ed	fee____ing	remi____ion

Spelling rule

When there is a short vowel sound ending in a single consonant, you double the consonant before adding the suffix.

sit ⟶ sitting

rot ⟶ rotten

Activity 2

Using the spelling rule above, say each root word and listen to the sounds to help you decide when the consonant needs to be doubled in these verbs.

Root	add **ing**	add **ed**
shop		
drop		
hope		
beg		
love		
train		

Activity 3

Use the words in the list to complete the sentences.

puzzle   dropping   hidden   trodden   attached

a) I have _____ my sweets from my brother!

b) I have _____ in some mud.

c) The difficult jigsaw _____ has over 3000 pieces.

d) She _____ a photograph to her email.

e) Mariah kept _____ the ball in netball today.

Investigate!

Use some of the words from this unit to create clues for others to solve.

16 Homophones and near-homophones

Homophones are words that sound very similar but are spelled differently and mean different things.

A near-homophone is two words that sound very similar, but are spelled differently.

peas and **peace**
there and **their**

Activity 1

Match the pairs of **homophones** below. One has been done for you.

advice	father
licence	guest
farther	herd
guessed	license
practice	advise
heard	practise

Activity 2

Can you write the missing meanings to these homophones?

aloud	to speak so that others can hear
allowed	_____
morning	the period of time between midnight and noon
mourning	_____
serial	_____
cereal	a grain used for food
alter	to change something
altar	_____

Activity 3

Choose the correct homophone or
near-homophone to complete each sentence.

a) I _____ him in the road. (passed/past)

b) I had a _____ after my main course.
(desert/dessert)

c) There was a _____ coming from the window. (draught/draft)

d) The _____ problem was the lack of time. (principal/principle)

e) We were _____ in the car as it had broken down. (stationary/
stationery)

f) The metal we used was _____. (steel/steal)

g) After the match, the players were very _____. (weary/wary)

h) The girl made a polite _____ about the lady's dress. (compliment/
complement)

Activity 4

Match each word to its definition.

proceed	an invited person
precede	to go ahead
guest	the result of something
guessed	to go before
affect	to have estimated something
effect	to have an influence on

Investigate!

Can you write a paragraph containing incorrect homophones for others to
change to the correct word?

17 Adding prefixes and suffixes

A prefix is added to the beginning of a root word. When you add a prefix to a root word, you change the word's meaning.

Here are some common prefixes and their meanings.

re = again, back   **mis** = wrong

dis = not   **pre** = before

un = not, opposite   **under** = below

Activity 1

Write the correct prefix next to each root word.

a) _____play   to play again

b) _____age   below age

c) _____print   to print incorrectly

d) _____able   not able

e) _____heat   to heat before

f) _____wind   to wind back or again

g) _____honest   not honest

h) _____treat   to treat wrongly

i) _____tied   not tied

j) _____water   below the water

k) _____happy   not happy

l) _____view   to view before

Spelling rule

A suffix is added to the end of a root word. When you add a suffix to a root word, you change the word's meaning.

Here are some common suffixes and their meanings.

able = can be done

est = most

ful = full of

less = without

er = more

er = one who

Activity 2

Choose and write the correct word from the list next to its meaning.

joyful   careless   slower   youngest

readable   worthless   teacher   singer   doable

a) Able to read   _____

b) More slow   _____

c) One who teaches   _____

d) Without care   _____

e) Full of joy, with joy   _____

f) Most young   _____

g) Without worth   _____

h) One who sings   _____

i) Able to be done, able to do   _____

Investigate!

How many different words with the prefixes and suffixes used in these activities can you find in your favourite book?

18 Stress in words

Stresses in words enable us to read them correctly and also give us clues about spelling patterns when adding prefixes and suffixes.

The meaning of the word can change depending upon which syllables we stress. An example of this is the word **present**.

- If we stress the first syllable, it says **pre**-sent (a gift).
- However, if we stress the second syllable, it becomes pre-**sent** (to hand over or give).

Activity 1

Read each word and say it aloud. Copy the words and circle the part of each word where you can hear the stress.

a) computer

b) hotel

c) Saturday

d) hospital

e) hairbrush

f) respect

g) lagoon

h) witness

i) trumpet

j) begin

k) visit

l) football

Activity 2

Copy the table into your book and sort the words in the list below according to their stressed syllable.

winter   acceptance   breakfast   respect   eminent   absolute

afternoon   examine   employer   policeman   herself   report

First syllable stressed	Second syllable stressed	Third syllable stressed

Spelling rules

When you add suffixes to words with more than one syllable that end in a single consonant after a vowel, you need to think where the stress lies.

- If the stress is on the second syllable, you follow the rule for doubling the last consonant

  begin ⟶ **beginner/beginning**

- If the stress is on the first syllable, words ending in **l** double the last letter.

  travel ⟶ **traveller**

  However, words ending in **t** don't double.

  visit ⟶ **visited**

Activity 3

Use the spelling rules above to fill in the past tense for each of these verbs.

limit	limited
commit	
panel	
visit	
remit	
trumpet	
refer	
transfer	
fulfil	
level	

19 Etymology and word families

There are groups of words that are based on the same root word, but they have different prefixes or suffixes. Looking at these, you will notice how the word can be made into different word classes and also change its meaning. Thinking about these word families can help you to spell them, as they will follow a pattern.

act, actor, action, react, reaction

The root word is **act** – all of the other words are made from **act**.

Activity 1

Copy the table into your book and add other words to these word families.

child	electric	take
childish		

Activity 2

Find the root word for each of these families.

a) re-educate, education, educator _____

b) disappear, reappear, appeared, appearing _____

c) accessed, accesses, accessibility, accessible _____

d) created, creating, creation, recreate, creators _____

e) designer, designing, designed, designers _____

Activity 3

Copy the table into your book and sort the words in the list into the correct word families.

imbalance   recall   forgiveness   enjoyment   disobey   given

impress   shaken   heroic   cooperation   approval   relation

joyful   unbalanced   depression   cooperate   relative

call	
obey	
prove	
operate	
give	
balance	
joy	
shake	
press	
hero	
relate	

Activity 4

Use each of these words in a sentence.

a) dedicate

b) dedication

c) improve

d) improvement

e) inform

f) information

Investigate!

Can you think of three root words and then write a list of other words that are related?

20 Word lists

Here are some of the words that you are expected to understand and be able to spell in Year 5.

accommodate	definite	privilege
accompany	desperate	profession
according	dictionary	pronunciation
aggressive	disastrous	occupy
ancient	embarrass	occur
apparent	environment	opportunity
appreciate	exaggerate	recommend
attached	explanation	secretary
available	familiar	signature
bruise	foreign	soldier
category	government	sufficient
cemetery	identity	suggest
committee	immediate	symbol
communicate	marvellous	system
community	nuisance	thorough
competition	parliament	vegetable
correspond	physical	

Activity 1

Practise writing and spelling the following words.

Write	Look Cover Say Check
community	
nuisance	
sufficient	
attached	
committee	

Activity 2

Only one spelling in each set is correct. Decide which one you think it is and then use a dictionary to check.

a) acomodate accomodate accommodate   _____

b) soldier solder soldear   _____

c) vegitable vegetable vegetible   _____

d) imediate immediate imidiate   _____

e) signature signeture signiture   _____

f) compitition competition competision   _____

g) simbol symbol symble   _____

h) opportunity opotunety opportnety   _____

i) recomend reccommend recommend   _____

Activity 3

Use each of these words in a sentence to show its meaning.

a) parliament

b) nuisance

c) accompany

d) convenience

e) familiar

f) disastrous

g) privilege

h) exaggerate

Investigate!

Use the list on page 35 to test your spelling with your friends and family.

21 Using a dictionary and thesaurus

Dictionary

A dictionary is a very useful tool. It helps us to spell a word correctly, find out the word class of a word and it explains the meaning of a word. All dictionaries use alphabetical order to organise the words.

Palm noun **palms** 1. The inside part of your hand. 2. A palm tree is a tree that is grown in hot climates.

Pan noun **pans** 1. A metal pan that you could use for cooking food in.

Pancake noun **pancakes** 1. A flat cake that is made out of flour, eggs and milk.

Panda noun **pandas** 1. A large bear that is black and white.

Pane noun **panes** 1. A piece of glass is called a pane of glass.

Panic verb **panics**, panicking, panicked 1. When you suddenly feel very frightened and cannot think what to do you are panicked.

Pantomime noun **pantomimes** 1. A play that is performed at Christmas time which has jokes and songs in.

Paper noun **papers** 1. Paper is a material you can draw or write on. 2. Another word for a newspaper.

Parachute noun **parachutes** 1. A safety tool used when flying which opens up over your head to stop you from falling too quickly.

Parade noun **parades** 1. A long group of people marching or walking through a crowd.

Paragraph noun **paragraphs** 1. A section of a longer piece of writing.

Parcel noun **parcels** 1. An object that is wrapped up and sent to another person.

Parent noun **parents** 1. A parent is a mother or father.

Park noun **parks** 1. A large space, usually covered with grass, where people can walk or play.

Park verb **parks**, **parking**, **parked** 1. When you need to leave your car you park it in a space.

Parliament noun **parliaments** 1. The group of people who make the laws and important decisions for a country.

Activity 1

Use the information above to answer the following questions.

a) What type of word is the word **parade**?

b) What does the word **parliament** mean according to this dictionary?

c) Where would the word **parchment** fit on this page?

d) Can you write a definition to go with the word **parchment**?

e) What type of word is the word **pair**?

f) Why does the word **palm** have two different definitions?

Thesaurus

We use a thesaurus to find other words that have a similar meaning to a word, or that have the opposite meaning (antonyms). We can use these words to make our writing more interesting. A thesaurus will also tell us the word class of a word and is organised in alphabetical order.

Activity 2

Use a thesaurus from the classroom to find other words that have similar meanings to the words listed below.

a) sad _____

b) nice _____

c) bright _____

d) sleepy _____

e) walk _____

f) eat _____

Activity 3

Use a thesaurus to find the word underlined and replace it with an appropriate synonym.

a) Jack did an <u>excellent</u> piece of work at school on Monday.

b) The teacher was <u>exhausted</u> after the first day at school.

c) The flower had a lovely <u>smell</u>.

d) The dog was very <u>quick</u> as it chased the cat.

e) I am going to <u>release</u> the bird tonight.

f) Mr Harrison is extremely <u>intelligent</u>.

Investigate!

Use a thesaurus to change some of the words in your own writing.

22 Idioms

An idiom is a phrase that does not mean what the words actually say.

It cost me an arm and a leg.

This idiom means it was very expensive rather than the item was paid for with body parts!

Activity 1

Write down the meaning of each idiom and then use it correctly in a sentence.

a) a piece of cake

b) pass the buck

c) lend him a hand

d) down to earth

e) sounds like a broken record

f) think outside the box

g) hold on a second

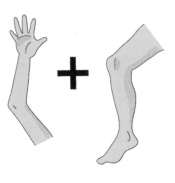

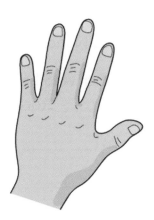

Activity 2

Match each idiom to its meaning.

Idiom	Meaning
Don't add fuel to the fire!	It's good to save money, rather than spending it and wasting it.
A penny saved is a penny earned.	Something is imagined; not real.
Around the clock.	Don't make a bad situation even worse.
A picture is worth a thousand words.	Being away from someone you love makes your love even stronger.
It's all in your head!	All of the time; 24 hours a day.
Absence makes the heart grow fonder.	Pictures can give more information than just words.

Activity 3

Use the idioms in the list to complete the sentences.

from rags to riches   **fixed in her ways**   **get over it**

go for broke   **go out on a limb**   **gut feeling**

a) I couldn't decide if I should go for the part in the play, but my aunt said,
"_____."

b) We had hoped Nana would get cable TV but she is _____.

c) The dish washer, who became an overnight singing sensation, is a
_____ story.

d) I am going to _____ and say that I think it may rain today.

e) I had a _____ it was a surprise party.

f) I was pretty upset that my brother took my bicycle, but my mum told me to just
_____.

Investigate!

Use the internet and books from the classroom to find other common idioms.
Write a list for others to use.

23 Antonyms

Antonyms are words that mean the opposite of one another, such as **good** and **bad**.

- Some antonyms can be made with the prefixes **anti, un, in, im, non, il** and **dis**.

  climax ⟶ anti-climax   important ⟶ unimportant

  appropriate ⟶ inappropriate   mature ⟶ immature

  fiction ⟶ non-fiction   legal ⟶ illegal

  respectful ⟶ disrespectful

- Some antonyms can be made with the suffix **less**.

  meaning ⟶ meaningless

- Most antonyms are just different words.

  enormous ⟶ minuscule

Activity 1

Copy these lists of **adjectives**. Join up the opposites in each list.

fat	sad	heavy	strong
long	hard	far	slow
happy	thin	big	near
narrow	dry	weak	light
wet	short	noisy	small
soft	wide	fast	quiet

Activity 2

Make antonyms from the words below by adding one of these prefixes.

un   dis   im   in   non   mis

Word	Antonym
comfortable	
active	
possible	
sense	
sufficient	
behave	
fiction	
believe	
patient	

Activity 3

Write as many antonyms as you can think of for each of the words below.

a) big

b) dull

c) young

d) sad

e) stop

f) dirty

g) gleam

h) play

i) joke

Activity 4

Match each word from the orange box with its antonym in the blue box.

create   rush   incomplete   terminate   thorough   thwart

convenient   vigilant   hateful   departure   disastrous   success

a) commence

b) assist

c) lovable

d) destroy

e) disaster

f) fortunate

g) careless

h) inconvenient

i) complete

j) inattentive

k) arrival

l) dawdle

Most antonyms are not exact opposites, as shades of meaning are involved – as with synonyms (a word that means the same or nearly the same). A thesaurus is a useful tool for finding both antonyms and synonyms.

Investigate!

Can you use some of the antonyms to create clues for others to solve?

24 Word meaning

It is important that when we are writing we use words that are creative and thought-provoking for the reader. However, we must ensure that we use vocabulary in the correct context. Therefore, it is very important to use a dictionary to check the meanings of words to ensure our sentences makes sense.

Activity 1

Tick the words closest in meaning to:

a) dispute

	Tick one
agreement	
achievement	
mishap	
quarrel	

b) surprise

	Tick one
astonishing	
nice	
predictable	
expected	

c) certainly

	Tick one
actually	
definitely	
possibly	
soon	

Draw a line from the word on the left to the word on the right that means the **opposite**.

a)

contrasting	deceiving
	different
	long-lasting
	similar

b)

enemy	foe
	arch-enemy
	ally
	fiend

c)

brave	cowardly
	courageous
	bold
	energetic

d)

rough	twisted
	tough
	textured
	smooth

e)

laugh	howl
	chuckle
	cackle
	cry

Investigate!

When reading a book, use a dictionary to look up the true meaning of any words you are unsure of.

25 Vocabulary in context

Context clues are words or phrases in a sentence that help us work out the meaning of an unfamiliar word. Often, you can figure out the meanings of new or unfamiliar vocabulary by paying attention to the surrounding language.

Activity 1

Find a word that can complete **both** sentences in each pair of sentences.

a) You should remember to look both ways before you_____ the road.

Adam was very _____ that he couldn't play at the park.

b) I need to get some money from the _____.

The ducks live on the _____ beside the river.

c) Please don't take any more chips _____ my plate!

You will need to read _____ page 1 to page 9 to answer the questions.

Activity 2

Circle the best word in the list to replace the underlined word in each sentence.

a) The man was <u>angry</u>. (irritated, irate, initiate, initial)

b) Joe's <u>apparel</u> was colourful. (picture, pasta, clothing, pet)

c) Charlie was <u>yearning</u> for her dad. (waiting, working, performing, longing)

d) Rio was <u>garrulous</u>. (talkative, greedy, tired, gorgeous)

e) The dog was <u>wary</u>. (war-like, worried, nervous, cautious)

Each sentence has context clues to help you figure out the meaning of the underlined word. Read the sentences carefully for the context clues and choose the correct meaning of each underlined word.

a) The long hike up to the top of the mountain was extremely <u>gruelling</u>.

loud/tiring/easy

b) The <u>conspicuous</u> man wore a purple wig and large sunglasses.

easily noticed/beautiful/sleeping

c) I was so <u>parched</u>, I drank an entire glass of water in one go.

hungry/thirsty/sleepy

d) The delightful <u>aroma</u> of food cooking in the kitchen made my mouth water.

smell/colour/wealth

e) The car park was so <u>congested</u>, it took half an hour to get out!

empty/hot/crowded

f) India is a <u>novice</u> netball player; it's her first day of practice.

skilled/beginner/professional

g) Jordan was <u>envious</u> of his brother's new bike.

jealous/confident/comfortable

Investigate!

Can you find out what the following words mean: tenacious, mendacious, alluring, ambiguous? Use them in a sentence correctly.

Word lists

Here is a list of words you will need to be familiar with in Year 5. Some of them have tricky spellings which you will need to learn.

unstressed vowels

(Year 5)

accommodate

bruise

category

cemetery

definite

desperate

dictionary

embarrass

environment

exaggerate

marvellous

nuisance

parliament

privilege

secretary

vegetable

'i' before 'e' except after 'c' when the sound is ee

(Year 6)

achieve

convenience

mischievous

'i' before 'e' only

(Year 5)

soldier

sufficient (exception to the rule)

variety

ancient (exception to the rule)

foreign (exception to the rule)

double consonants

(Year 5)

accommodate

accompany

according

aggressive

apparent

appreciate

attached

committee

communicate

community

correspond

immediate

occupy

occur

opportunity

recommend

suggest

suffixes and prefixes

(Year 6 review)

according

attached

criticise (criticise)

determined

equip(-ment, -ped)

especially

frequently

immediate(-ly)

(un)necessary

sincere(-ly)

tion words

(Year 5)

competition

explanation

profession

pronunciation

ough letter strings

(Year 5)

thorough

word families

(Year 5)

familiar

identity

signature

symbol

(this is revision from Year 3)

'y' makes the 'i' as in *bin* sound

(Year 5)

physical

symbol

system

(this is revision from Year 3)

'c' makes *s* sound before 'i', 'e' and 'y'

(Year 6)

cemetery

convenience

criticise

excellent

existence

hindrance

necessary

prejudice

sacrifice

ous words

(Year 5)

disastrous

unstressed consonants

(Year 5)

government

words originating from other countries

(Year 5 and 6)

conscience

conscious

desperate

yacht

crosscurricular words

(Years 5 and 6)

forty

temperature

twelfth

le words

(Year 5)

available

other words

(Years 5 and 6)

amateur

average

awkward

bargain

controversy

curiosity

develop

forty

guarantee

harass

hindrance

identity

individual

interfere

interrupt

language

leisure

lightning

muscle

neighbour

persuade

programme

queue

recognise

relevant

restaurant

rhyme

rhythm

shoulder

signature

stomach

temperature

twelfth

vegetable

vehicle

yacht